A JANUARY AFTERNOON
and
Other Poems

A January Afternoon

and

Other Poems

Anne Noland

Norman S. Berg, Publisher

"Sellanraa," Dunwoody, Georgia

1973

This is an edition of one thousand copies of which nine hundred and fifty copies are for sale.

ISBN 910220-53-0

For Mop

Contents

I

II

Anne Noland; A January Afternoon

I

A January Afternoon

I know that you loved
Mozart.
And this afternoon,
while from a crowded
shopping center
we were at last coming
home,
we heard his name through
the music being played
on a F.M. station.
Our nerves were soothed,
there was now lovely,
white snow on the ground
and stretches of clear
sky with tall, quiet pines,
our eyes grew heavy.
Just then I thought of you,
for I remember too you
always having such trouble
falling asleep.
I wished that we had taped
some Mozart,
so that at night sleep
might have drifted more
easily into your room.
Though, perhaps, your mind
had become so confused
that night or no music at all
could have made the day

at last restful for you.
I pray now the one true Genius
who writes the ode of Spring
that you hear him playing
and that you are sleeping
gently.

At The Water's Edge

At the water's edge
our house grew.
I was led to the shore,
when only three,
to play upon the warm
earth sand,
the river's lap;
which when she pulled
back her rippling skirt,
a petticoat of foam
tied lace
held pretty treasures
beneath.
And in her lap
that stretched to a
kingdom far beyond,
I could build castles,
through which I never
searched,
because she was impatient
and shifted her knees.
It was fine, though,
child-napped
against the thin, shell
breast of a queen -
her crown
the sinking sun.
And I as a small sea
bird,

knowing her touch
as the silken
stroke
of lullaby moon
hands.

Annis

Her arms forever clasped
in a round circle
mimicing the sun,
time and energy for
everything.

Her day giving glow
tore only once
when then she wept
for the death of a friend,
her father,
her blue sky.

To Sylvia Plaith

You stood once
with golden
plaits,
ropes of promise
tied about
your neck.

You saw things
then as a child
poet,
your pheasant in
the woods
"a little cornucopia".

Slowly, you loosened
your braids,
trusting a man
running his fingers
through your hair,
free.

Suddenly, you learned
his touch
as a pusher of
nightmares,
hardened dreams,
leaving you

Bare and bruised
as barreled
fruit
in the
morning light.

Split and without
seed,
an empty mouthful,
in the
hungry night.

"Morning Song"
sculptor unknown

Undoubtedly,
a winter's morning.
Vermont marble
the cast of
bare December skies.
A mother with
her child
held close,
tucked between the
other's trust,
huddled near the
hearth.
The stone eases
slowly
to warmth—
a song suddenly
in prasie
of deep snow,
swaying
outside.

In Memory of J.A.

Once
there was a
teacher,
who baked his own
bread
and so delicately
ignited
the readiness
of all
things,
including
me.

Songs of Fairy Dust

I can't spin
those exquisite
songs of fairy
dust
leaving morning
in the minds
of those who
come to my
doors
at night.

I have not
lived
under the
doom
of Beauty
who slept
awakened
just in time
by a prince.

I admit
that mostly
I have
survived
the time
of a child
knowing not
a beginning

nor expecting
a life
that lives ever
after.

I dream
just
to play
before your eyes
in fingerpaints
the brillant
potion
of this sun-
spilled
day.

Snail-Like

What makes
people
snail-like
crawling
along
so close
to the
ground
dragging
their hearts
a tight
little
shell?

For My Mother

I am sure it
was the same
years ago,
when your father,
my grandfather,
took you by the hand,
calling you his little
Jenny Wren,
and you gazed for the
first time at the
blue of Robin eggs
in the Spring.
Had someone painted
them that way
just for Easter time,
you asked;
and who hid them
then in the brown
nest?
The mother bird
seemed to know,
the color of them
she liked.
Little, fragile
forget-me-nots
her Robin man
had left.
Their sweet, warm

fragrance
only she beheld,
within her
home
ground.

It Was Not You

It was not you
that I wanted
or so badly needed.
I was satisfied
with the bare
tree branches
that are
against
the lonely, grey
skies
of winter.
But it
is you
who have brought
flights
of songbirds
to amuse the
clouds
and you
who whisper
to the leaves
to dance
inside
my head.

Seagulls

It is your time
of day too.
As I come strolling along
the sea wall,
in a dawn colored gown,
because it floats
and I feel more like one
of you,
gliding in the early
morning air.
I have not been threatened
by people,
so I'm free;
feeling not awkward in a
long laced robe,
for it serves the day
and you,
my morning gulls well.
There is now only the sound
of oyster boats,
solid white waves,
upon the far horizon.
You have decided to ride
the moveable ones in,
that toss secrets softly
into the ears of shells.
There is no use trying to
listen,
to gather information,

for all secrets are lost
in the course of conversation.
I'm glad then we do not speak
the same language,
but share the same shore.

From Mop's Room Months Afterwards

Across your empty bed,
looking beyond through
your window,
the river is swollen
grey, flooded with
tears.
I thought our grief
was unbearable,
so heavy I was unable
to move from an armchair
for days.
But now as I gaze
upon this bruised heart,
wide with sorrow,
I ache for its discomfort
alone.
It is not an angry
father,
ready to spank the
world dropping at its
feet.
Today, it tells the story
of a mother moaning,
unable to find her child,
fallen from her arms.
There is not a pray of peace
in her roaming, tumultuous
questions why.

Only when the skies clear,
and by chance,
she lifts her sagging
eyelids,
will she ever find her child
again.

Friends of Cinderella

I am not sure who set the birds
loose this year.
They have come from some fine
toymaker's hands.
Crafted unusually small,
they perch light as a
four o'clock's song.
And are painted true
as the newest berries
propped on a winter's branch.
Though, it is their tiny manners
that are most polite;
certainly, some genius has
wound them up.
For they are like the creatures
that flew every dawn to
Cinderella's windows.
Tying back the sash of her curtains,
catching the threads of her apron;
soothing all the labors of her day,
by simply coming near,
smiling at her.

For Edward E. Cummings

e.e.
i,i
adore you.
the peach
blossoms
are
falling
silently
as the first
snow
it is
your time
of year
flower man
and all i can say
is how
i wish you
were here.

A Japanese Doll

If you took
this friend
in hand,
you would be
holding
a gift
so precious.
Her face
pale
as
the first
whisper of
lotus
blossom.
Her sweet
crystal
eyes
bluer
than what
the
Venetians
ever knew.
All this
held
within
a frame
so small
and running
more pure

inside
than what
Buddha
or even
Christ
hoped
children
to be.

Mid-October

This is a day
I choose for
my wedding,
an October
day,
the perfect
kind.
Birds stitched
to the underside
of sky,
as frail Oriental
eyes,
beating their
tiny
inspirations.
And gathered
farther beyond,
old friends
I have stood
with all my life,
who raise to
us now
a bold offering
in trust,
that Spring
returns again to
earth.

Spring Comes

Spring comes,
children with
towels as white
cloaks,
draped about
their narrow
shoulders.
Young Lancelots
treading
carefully
across green
grass.
Their vision
and mine
somehow as one,
the lavender sky
tells of a love
not yet
reckoned with.

For G.

Gusts of wind
bring your name
to mind.
Wanting before
a man soft
and even -keeled
as a time in May.
There is no person,
no man that can
possibly be.
Facing you,
I no longer
hold to the light
of dreams,
abrasive sands
blow now in my
face—
smooth and polished,
I will someday
lie in your
aftermath.

The Crab Factory

Crouched low
on the
waterfront,
a building
barnacled,
aged,
breathing
salt air
for seventy-
five years
past.
Through the
sticky,
summer screen
door,
nimble fingers
inside tug
sea flesh
from
shell bone.
And all
the while,
their laboring
of black
claws,
coming closer,
as though
I was the next
to be
skinned
alive.

For R.D.

Your hair
red,
balding
a bit;
just like
the
autumn
branch,
we passed
beneath.

You fear
so greatly,
this turning
of the
year;
I am
younger,
green
in fact—

I wish
we could
join
hands
and make
it
last.

Snow Fall

Madonna
grey sky,
a melancholy
eye
casted upon
this
tender world,
a child of
sorts.
Have you been
foretold
of our future
fate?
In a new,
warm
embrace,
you have
made
snow come
down
all around.
I know if
you had
your way,
all your children
would be
cradled in such
pure grace.
But your

eyes are sad,
while seeing us
in swadling
clothes,
you know we'll
outgrow.

An Elder Lady

Your beauty
is not
old,
it has
aged.
Something
turned
inside
out.
Tolerance
has
become
your
head dress.
The jewels
of your
crown,
shine now
upon my
youth.

Diane DiPrima

She who
married
and thought
less
of him
than
the old
coal
stove
keeping them
warm
through the
chill
winter months.
I can
see
her still
rubbing
her hands
before
its open, cast-
iron
mouth,
catching
the sparks
and turning
them
to poems
upon paper.

The words
still burn,
the pages
of her books
are singed.
And what
if she
had turned
to him
in the cold
still
silence
of night,
rather than
tend
her fierce,
strong
fire
of poem?

A Barely Met Acquaintance

I was waiting
for you
to write
me poems.
I forgot
that
is my
trade.
I ease
the anxiety
now inside
my heart.
I send
to you
quiet messages
of thought.

After Dining With Old Friends

The loft of bed holds me here,
at home, windows swung free to
the sea.

It can not be the tin of cow
bells, hammering afield, that
so faintly I hear.

Or a medieval steeple,
loosening its secrets from stone,
as midnight draws near.

I remember now, it is only
the drifting of hearts, anchored
safe and secure to the pier.

To George

You lying
frail as
a forsaken
Asian soldier,
knowing no
end to
misery.
Your bones
touching
your flesh,
touching
the thin
hospital sheets.
Though, you
are found
and visited
by us,
from comfortable
homes;
the pain
scratching your
sores,
tells tales
of a war
many miles
from here—
now it is
all so
real.

Boss

You who
have never
pushed,
bossed anyone.
To me
your
heart
wears the
gloss
of such deep
tranquil
depths.
For what
you would
say
as we sat
there,
in the doorway
of the
wooden stall.
Daddy was
still
out riding;
remember,
I would
come in early
because my hands
were cold
and I couldn't

hold back
the frightened
animal -
I was frightened
too,
you knew.
I was never
meant for
run-away stallions;
only your
kindness
which made me warm
again and safe inside.

St. Louis
April 12, 1972

After so many months
we all agreed
it was time for things
to be made all right,
that it was time we
saw the light.
And tonight after another
dark hospital's day,
we can hear the stars sigh
with relief.
We are too full of
gratitude
to ask for the sun's
strength
just yet.

Broadway, England

Lady Armitage

She described her own
as a kangaroo mind;
she had lived so long
by herself,
no wonder today,
as we sat before her,
she lept and bound
from one thought to
another.
But now and again,
she would light as
a butterfly,
stunned by some sweet
scent of memory—
her heart was still
full of flower.

In His Arms

I was tucked
in his arms
like
a child.
Though, his
touch
did more than
put me to
sleep—
my heart is
now still
awake.

A Way Not Known

I don't know
where to go
from here;
two paths
are not
evident from
which to choose,
one telling all
the right
difference.
I am in a wood,
I suppose,
but it is no
longer autumn;
the yellow drapes
have been removed
and now the walls
of only twigs,
hold not a
comforting sign.
I do not imagine
myself starting
out,
making brave
tracks through the
snow.
To the fire place
inside,
instead I'll turn,

kindling with care
some warm
future
glow.

The End Is Drawing Near

The end
is drawing
near,
my heart's
in my mouth,
it's quiet
hard to speak.
I'll just
place this
flower
in your hands,
goodbye.
Remember me,
though,
when the color
is gone,
when summer's
growth
has fallen
to autumn
and winter's
bleakness
has suddenly
blossomed
to Spring.
Remember me
when the
flowers
are around
again,
please.

My Life Is Full Of Pain

My life
is full
of pain

window
paines

I am
inside
myself

looking
out.

II

Poetess, Lace Words Up In Pretty Dress

What If

What if the sky were green
And grass blue?
What if birds sat still
And we flew?
What if the sun shed tears
And grey skies smiled?
What if there were really peace
And all our hearts with flowers
tiled?

November
New Hampshire 1969

The hills were as a blanket,
drawn over a dying body;
once quilted in vibrant shades,
only now dull of color.
There was no breathing,
silence lay beneath the bare
threads
cold and still.

Delicate Touch

Delicate touch –
draw flowers like
they grow;
thank you, Picasso.

Autumn

Tears of the earth
leaves falling down
the wrinkled faces of
time.

Gray Day

Gray day
the sun is lost
and so am I.
I hang myself
drip-dry
in a closet
of still wrinkled
thoughts.

Bird In Japanese Bush

Brown sparrow
parcel,
you are all
bundled
into this paper
pod tree,
waiting for
some fallen
leaf breeze
to come untie
your feathered
strings,
setting the last
pieces of
autumn hymns
free.

In A Dell

Lady slipper
song
to
Indian Pipes
white,
along the ground.

In A Forest Glen

Lightening bugs,
thousands of
tinkerbells,
signaling
the world
still
full of midnight
summer's
dream.

A Summer's Afternoon

A storm is coming,
it is sharp.
All the field
hands,
grass and flower,
soon to be
whipped for dancing
all the
afternoon
drunk
with sun.

Early Morning

The leaves new nudging
my consciousness,
pushing my mind to one side
open.
Whispering to remind me
to greet the day
carefully.

A November Midnight

The moon
tonight
glides
over frozen
snowfields
of cloud.

A silver
bloated
fish
dwifting upon
the cold waves
of sea sky.

An empress
who at
last has
turned
from the Great
Wall.

Her lonely
visions
reach
now
to enlighten
all.

September

The grass
dampened
with twlight's
falling,
made my feet
ache
for summer's
rising.

Crispin
butterflies
fallen
leaves.

Cold chill
that slipped
beneath
the curtain
and the edge of
the window
sill.

October

The flowers
hand
themselves
to the tops
of trees
returning
color
for borrowed
shade.

Dry, Brown Leaves

Hands
of the devil,
skeletonal
trees,
can't catch
me
with dying
interest.

Icicles

Glass stockings
hung from
the roof,
with hopes that
the sun
don't come
near.
Knowing then
the toes
would spill,
crystal
spears
of no
goodwill.

Robert Frost

Yes, you are now only
alive in those seasons
that bear your mark—
frost, an elusive sign of poetness.

White lights
of
Christmas
time,
electric snow
flakes
falling
down.

Spring Dawn

When all the world is
emerging,
as an Easter Egg;
  drawn by
a tiny hand
from the purest
blue of dyes,
  then placed,
    dripping,
ever so carefully
upon the greenest nest
  of grass.

A Hummingbird

The tiny golden beak
slender as a queen's embroidering
needle
treads a flower's heart
the day's lightness
weaving a moment fine enough
to examine the jewels
of your eyes against.

Lying On A Bank
Toward A Wood

The sun sets back
into the big oak cupboard;
behind the fine blue china
of day washed pale by this
hour.
The clouds we had were good;
feeling now as new-borns,
jugs of milk fed,
we are content.
While the tilt of grass
rocks slow to sleep
and the doors of the forest
quietly latch.

Dusk of Winter

The lean
bare
forms,
stepping forth
from
a warm
tub.

Wrapped now
in soft
towels
of
grey
soothing
mist.

Reaching
ever
so slowly
for
their
black velvet
robes

To seduce the night.

The Arno, Florence
February 1972

Upon the winter, barren river
a swan floats,
pulling behind a silvering
strand of hope.

Her mate will never be again,
but in gracious remorse
how softly she
draws the way for Spring.

Winter Trees

Empty handed,
no more golden
pennies to hold,
their feeble fingers
yearn for the
offering plate
of sun;
passed by a Priest
in blue satin.
Though, as it fades
farther and farther
from reach,
the taste suddenly
of a cold, endless
sky is
insufferable.
Against their
starved
tongues.

First Day of Winter
Willaimsburg

How authentic
in this
village,
the trees bundled
as hand-crafted
broomsticks,
set against a
dusty, grey sky.
I wait for
wide black arms
to gather them
up,
sweeping the
rafters bare
above our heads,
while snow white
doves fly
out.

September Kindergarden

Scattered along
the ancient,
crooked
sidewalk,
children
on a kite
string
flutter.
Their new,
brightly
colored woolens,
any twig
would be
only too
glad to
snag.

Hyde Park
January 1972

The trees lost of their gold,
now glimpsed so pale through
thin forests' depths,
are full of faith still.
They do not pinch pockets.
With arms raised upward,
poverty etched meekly for all to see,
they pray knowingly for wealth to return.
When the sky's chalice pours
warm once more.

Tiny Black Child

Tiny black
child
like
a small brown
top
twirling twirling
to the
tinkling cheers
of all
sprawled merrily
summer
upon the tall
green grasses
sipping
lemon
warm
sun.

To A Grieving Spider

A spider
father
fumbles
over an ant
child's
body,
turning all
the legs of
sorrow,
looking for
a secret.
Emptiness,
though,
has no edges;
like a web
you weave,
dying stretches
clear –
though,
unresolved
into the
night.

Sargent Mountain, Maine

Here above the
timber line,
the same as in
New York City—
though, there
are no people.
The stone flats,
barren and cold,
house not a leaf
of green.
And I am close
enough to the
clouds to speak.
But today,
grim-faced,
they too rush passed
with no kind words.

New Orleans, La.

The dawn
crept in upon
while linen wings
tilting shadows of
light
to abolish the
night.
I awaken now in
peace
as if an angel hovered
close and whispered
yes
to this our first
drawing day.

A Night In Late Autumn

Fairy
godmother,
when are you
going
to set your
harvest
moons rolling?
Pumpkins
into carriages
to cart all
autumn color
away.
So that
in the frost
filled morning,
the fields
left lonely
can appreciate
fully
your snow stars
dumped upon
them.

After "Songs of Innocence"

The Sun

Little sun, who made thee?
Dost thou know who made thee?
Gave thee light and bid thee warmth
through the day and beneath the night.
Little sun, who made thee?
Dost thou know who made thee?

Little sun, I'll tell thee
Little sun, I'll tell thee
For He is bright and He is strong
He calls Himself the Son.
I a star and thou the sun
We are called by His name.

Little sun, God bless you.
Little sun, God bless you.

Found Today Under A Tree

Golden buckeye,
you have the very
finest luster of
mahogany.
Though, better
than a table
or some chair,
you sit
in my palm.
Feeling you there
is like
having a good
friend
in for tea.